Words In a Row:
Book One
2nd Edition

Words In A Row:
Book One
2nd Edition

D. L. McClung

Re'el De'el Books
2014

First printing 2014

ISBN: 978-0692285725

Re'el De'el Books
272 Four States Road
Worthington, WV 26591

The Early Poems

Poems I wrote back when I was young and gave a damn. And a few new ones.

For

All the girls

I loved in vain

and all the lust

unsatisfied

If only there had been the time

and I had had the mind

that I have now and age were not

I would have done a better thing

and all that missed be rectified

And

Loves now missed

1.

Does anyone see the sky?
The lover or the wilted flower?
The Birds or the baby's tears?
Does anyone see the sky?

2.

This morning an old woman
ragged and worn
came to the doorway of her hut
She stared with dreamless eyes at passers-by
and swept away the dust.

Tomorrow an old woman
ragged and worn
with dreamless eyes
will sweep away the dust from her doorway
and stare at passers-by.

3.

Would you dare pretend if
ever once I looked at you and
saw the innocence you keep concealed
behind your mask of stone?
Would you?

4.

While a solitary cry
falls on deaf ears
somewhere love grows weak
because it cannot hear...

5.

The gentle breeze caressed her
as she lay upon the beach
and the arm of the ocean
stretched its hand but could not reach

The moonlight shined down on her
lying there upon the sand
and some proud forsaken lover
was the one who held her hand

And the night air smelled of death
from the wilted rose that lay
held by a blood stained hand
on the beach of Murder Bay...

6.

Hopefully a speck of dust is more intent
upon reaching nowhere and going far
than all the vain pursuits of Man
who dance the hollow halls
to vacant songs

7.

Eyes, black, blue, hazel, green,
don't reflect all that they have seen
only what they remember

8.

I loved her once but don't no more
She slapped my face and slammed the door

9.

Night came like a coffin closing
and shut me in
The cold settled
like a shroud concealing
all that was death
and I wept
My tears fell
painfully upon the hands
that held my head
I was alone
but agony kept its strength
and stayed with me until the end
The morning came
like angels singing
but I was gone...

10.

I saw them sitting, holding hands,
on a park bench, night.
The moon was bright and full.
Their lips united in a kiss
made them more than just friends.
She was young, beautiful, ideal in my eyes.
He was older, strong, handsome
brought my own frailty to mind.
Who am I?
Together, they, nameless, as only two lovers
in the night of the city could be
escaped my view
slipped into the shadows
and made themselves happier than I
could ever be...alone

11.

Piss on you
you nasty girl
I've had enough of you
Go away and leave me be
I don't love you any more
You're just a spoiled little girl
and frankly you're a bore

12.

The first half stands tall
meaningful in the clearing
and some, just below the Sun
content to contemplate, watch
as creeping fetters encompass
the base of eternity.
They, knowing all and fearless
neglect the compensations allowed them.
Yet I, wandering,
forfeit the clarity of contentment
the pity of consideration
The pain of knowledge and fearlessness
and accumulate the spirit of life
and gain a fortune in memories
and a second beginning

13.

There was a girl with auburn hair
and a smile that melted me
I would have done most anything
if she had only asked
I wanted her to live with me

I would have loved her well
and given her a diamond ring
and forgot about the past
But she had other plans
plans not including me

14.

Such disappointments we know well
there's no excuse to say
but in the end we all can tell
tomorrow's just another day...

15.

She said to me
she said to me
she said these words to me

Always and forever, I promise
And I'm not going anywhere, I swear
and, of course, I love you
I really really do
then she was gone...

16.

Damn your eyes, you lied to me
and I'm the fool for believing you
I took your word, I had faith in you
you broke my heart, you made me blue
I can't believe what you did to me
after all I did for you

17.

Words are just words
they mean what they mean
except when they don't
and are not what they seem

And I am certain of this
just how would I say it
words being what they are
I'm on to their shit

What I mean to say
is that words can be used
and used all proper
or miss-used and abused

I've found that it's true
but people refuse to See
when I tell them the truth
they won't believe me

Now how can that be
it's just English I speak
I say it quite well
it's truth that I seek
I want to be clear
and say the things that I know
so that they may See
and by Seeing they grow

Now words are just words
and they mean what they mean
so why can't they see that
and see what I've seen

I write some words
and put them in lines
and say what I mean
with wordy designs
It's not really clear
the people are confused
I say what I say
and incredibly abused

I wonder sometimes
the worth of it all
if telling the truth
is worth taking the fall

Now I just can't imagine
after suffering the blow
it being very smart
to keep putting words in a row

And yet I do
and I'm happier for it
tho the words fall on deaf ears
and I'm treated like shit

A poet, a bard
a singer of rhyme
an enigma, a muse
a passer of time

A teller of stories
a jokester, a card
sometimes quite amusing
but always the Bard
I think in rhythm
I speak in rhymes

I write down the words
in a row of lines

That makes me a poet
I suppose that it's so
I put words in a line
words in a row
I put words in a line
I put words in a row

18.

What does the world do with fools like me
who fall in love when love is not the game?
Why do the hearts of men seek out and win
the hearts that I myself had wished to claim?

Where does the heartsick lover go
to find the love that he must know?
Where in this world can he find
a place to hide and peace of mind?

19.

Red flags hang half high
blue flags drenched in blood
proudly flying they mark the sky
for soldiers lost and battles won.
Ghosts of soldiers walk the fields
bloody fields
lovers once
but are no more
War has made them still
War does make them still...

20.

The sky is black and tells no man the answers.
The stars possess no thrill of being seen
the blood drenched earth will never ponder
carelessly again
the possibilities

21.

Afterthought

I gave him life and he wanted more
a world and he was not content
love and a way to love
and he denied me
knowledge and he ridiculed me
I gave him death
and he forgot me...

22.

What you see in the mirror
is not you...
what the mirror sees
is you.

23.

In my youth I dreamed of rubbing bellies with a
perfumed girl
duty free
who in her nakedness would not be ashamed
of intimate postures
which we would devise

who would go one step beyond emotion
and practice her divine sensations
without restraint or shame
Who would care no more than I
how indecent seeming were our joys
which we would exploit to their limits
even if it meant the end
of living separately

24.

I do not know him
he is a stranger to me
He has secrets that long to be told
but I cannot tell them
his eyes glare into infinity
or penetrate the souls around him
He seems to know what he sees
and yet I wonder...

25.

Essence of ferment
slithering through the backbones of civilized savages
corrugated nothingness
trains of tanks, bombs, guns, planes, drones
soldiers
Vapor of ignorance
Total annihilation
impersonal extinction of one world madly
craving infinite death
by means no longer myth
doom immemorial
canonized bodies
sprinkled liberally around the fireball rotating

26.

Wouldn't it be wise
to look the other way
and never look into her eyes
if lies are all she has to say?

27.

In some infinite cloud of dreams I love her
yet who could not
Youth and beauty's gift belong to few so dear
White gowns hold her as I would
caress her as I wish I could
and purple slippers kiss her feet
Golden hair holds my gaze
I crave to touch its smooth and flowing strands
It lays as Holy Grace's crown upon the neck
of Nature's Queen
Words whispered as true love's song
from faithful lips
I cannot forget
And some hidden flame sparks
the gentle eyes
eyes that seem to see
and yet do not...

28.

It's not that I'm all nasty,
or take things too personal
and I really don't get all pissed off
at people for being a dick...
it's just that words are the tools of my trade
and I use them very well.

The fact of the matter is, my friend,
I use them like a stick...
to beat those babbling fools...
and give the rest some hell...

29.

What kind of fool you take me for
I'm not that kind at all
I never would bring harm to you
or cause you to trip and fall
I'm fair and just and rather nice
I've never done you harm
so why do you slander me
and attack me for my charm

Am I hurtful
am I rude
did I cause you pain
Have I ever once
used you for selfish gain

Do I play at silly games
or try to make you cry
I swear I've never lied to you
cross my heart and hope to die

Why would you treat me so
and call me all those names
when all I ever did
was love you thru your games
I'm not about to beg and plead
I'm done, I quit, you're not the one I need

30.

If I could be fifteen again just like I am today
I wouldn't hesitate to do it differently
I would do it another way

31.

Sweetness-
by Kathy also known
rests her head upon a velvet pillowed throne
as near to me as breath is myne
a picture from an image sent serves as substitute
till flesh is flesh
and heaven meant
I am but a humble bard
with naught but heart and words
but as I lay my head this night
upon my pillow soft
her eyes will be the only light
to keep my soul aloft
and I will be the richest man
who ever took a bow
and even tho I won't...I can
sleep in peace...for now

32.

The song they sing
seems to ring
bitterly
in my ears
and about the place
making silent reason
un-attainably distant

Thus with raging wisdom
I rob the noisy congregation
of its dignity
by silently stealing away

33.

I wish I were a golden lavaliere
or silver pendant on your ear
or polished stone upon your chest
or tender touch upon your breast
I wish I were a gown of lace
or jaded crown upon your face
or priceless pearls around your cheek
or velvet slippers upon your feet
I wish I were a kiss once kissed
a smile once smiled and forever missed
before I sat to write these lines
before your eyes had met with myne
and only then to mend a heart once broke

34.

What have I done
that cost me this
What have I said
that turned your head
what in the world or out
could have caused this doubt
Is it a matter of deceit
or were there matters incomplete
tell me tell me heart of myne
tell me the tale
show me a sign

35.

I sleep but to wake upon another day
of searching for the precious lady
I laugh but to weep
for the lack of peace
and the love of the precious lady
I work but to play
at the game of love
in the arms of the precious lady
I sleep, I search, I laugh and I weep
I work, and play, yet I fail to find
the heart of the precious lady

36.

Vacant House to the Wind Coming Through a Broken
Window-

Unseen your breath stirs the dust
that has settled thick
upon the artifacts of the poor
lost occupants of my vacant womb
Your chilly draft awakening
the slumbering specks
and slapping them
from their sorry slumber posts
cleaning just the tops of sagging tables
one leg fallen
as you pass
vaporized essence of your power
strikes my walls and echoes silently
through halls and rooms
long lost to human presence
stand erect

before its walls collapse and form the bass
for a future home
Which in its own time
shall know emptiness and decay?

37.

I have turned their stove-pipe souls
into marshmallow cream, and
I have walked crisscross through their minds
leaving traces of insanity
in the muck of their brains
I have led them into the purple swamp
of wailing lights and neon souls
and all the time they knew
I was unreal
I have painted their chests with silver blades
and whispered crimson tales of doom into their hearts
and planted seeds of discontent
in their sterile wombs
and fed them thorns
from their Master's crown
and all the time they knew
I was unreal
I have plagued them and cursed them
I have deceived them
and watched them parish
I will feast on their memories
and dwell in their graves for eternity knowing
they were fools
and did not care
that I was unreal...

38.

It may be hard for you to understand
it's true that things are not so clear
but if you have some faith in me
I'll do my best and make it, dear
as good as it can be....
Considering all it's meant to be
and everything it's not
I can only hope to see
the love of what we've got...
and that will comfort me

39.

The cream has curdled in the pot
too much churning spoiled the milk
the Bull has turned to barnyard rot
kicking dung to show his ilk

The rancid stuff fills the air
the milk snake slides away
it makes the barn unfit to bear
the stench has turned the hay
The sun will set and then will rise
another day will come thru
the Bull will still strut wise
as if he has a clue

But in the end when all is done anew
the Bull is beef and leather pantaloons
the barn is fresh and milk is due
then butter made in the afternoons...

40.

The uselessness of war can be understood
in a child's impatient whimper and a widow's tear-
stained eyes
as they pass
if you look.

Wife, child.
Where in yesterday's fallen dreams
can be found tomorrow's hope?
have control over the land
Exploit the weak.
And tell them, the innocent,
that you meant them no harm

Master,
begin to rebuild a man blown to bits
maimed for life
made impotent.
Diminished.

Erase the memory of a husband,
father, once of flesh and bone
mind and soul
now of broken plans and scattered bones
Make a contentment where there once was Joy.
As if you can...

41.

He took the risk
just on a whim
then with a tear
they buried him

42.

I am
You are
We are   us.
God is
essence of me being
and you being   us
All is
essentially good
rather God
infinitely existing
and basically
all of it
plus
particularly you
and me
being   us.

43.

In my heart I know
and yet I wonder
if I should let myself
given what I ponder
even contemplate
what may come to be
however regrettably
the sorry end of me

44.

I hardly had a clue
I was very young back then
that it would come to this

and I would have to pay
for all that had come due
while I lived in sin
ignoring the abyss

45.

I broke a heart today
to save from breaking another
If either really knew
and asked me why I bother
the broken hearts would be
all three including me

46.

It never fails to baffle me
and cause me to lament
what it is with these crazy fools
and what's with their intent

Are they really all that dumb
or are they simply demented
why would they say such stupid things
and come off deeply jaded
Now I don't mind a man that's somewhat dull
and lacking in the social graces
but it really bothers me
when people act like mental cases

Take for one this guy I know
he just keeps on arguing
even though the facts relate
he doesn't know anything
It seems to me he's not too bright

but that is not my fault
he just won't let it go
and continues his assault

I suppose I should relent
and let him have his say
but what a stupid bore he is
on top of that he's gay

Now don't think I'm a homophobe
I'm anything but that
it's just the way he looks at me
besides he's really fat

Yes, I know, it's rude of me
to say he's fat and gay
but all in all and in the end
he has it wrong his way

You see it's not about his size
or how he waves his hands
or even how he walks around
or sits or even stands

I don't mind the clothes he wears
though his fashion lacks good taste
it's just he doesn't understand
his arguments are a waste

And I really can't be sure
if when I point this out
he even has a clue
the fool, the dupe, the lout

47.

What is the cause of your discontent
that makes my soul so twist and bent
I do not have evidence or clue
of why this evil charge is due
I only know from past excuse
that I cannot escape abuse
or ever be completely free
with you, my heart, inside of me...

48.

Tell me something wise my friend
and tell me only truth
Don't even think to lie to me
I'd think you were uncouth
Pretend that I am strong enough
to handle any thing
and say the worst of it
regardless of the sting

49.

Tell me tell me heart of myne
tell me the tale
show me a sign
What I done or said
indeed what is the awful truth
Have I done a dreadful act
a morbid deed, a devil's pact
Tell me tell me, heart of myne
tell me the tale, show me a sign

50.

If I but knew what I might know
in future days to come
would I be better off or not
and would I be as dumb

Would I take the chance
and would I even dare
or would I play it safe
and only pretend to care

A heart is somewhat fragile
in the early years
the boy in me naive
and gullible to fears
I guess it's fair to say
I'll know those things one day

51.

I have a love that I can't show
it must be hid away
It means the world to me
it's name I cannot say
It's not because of shame or guilt
or due to something bad
It's just that if I let myself
that love would drive me mad

52.

I don't believe you said that
you hurt my feelings bad
whatever were you thinking

to make me feel this sad

It doesn't really matter
as if you thought it did
I'm not some shallow fool
I'm not some foolish kid

What really really matters
if you should care to know
is not what you think I said
but what I care to show

53.

If I am a good and decent man
would it reasoned be
only natural and true
that good would come to me?
What in the end could become of me
if I neglect my heart
to that degree that I can't feel
when it is torn apart?
Now let me say a word or two
in my defense and pride
It wasn't me that lied to you
twas you to me that lied

D. L. McClung began writing poetry as a young teenager, and after five decades he has put those Words In A Row in book form. Modern technology that didn't exist back in those early days, before computers and the internet, has made it possible to publish his early poems at last. But certainly not least. As he continues to compose new poems, expressing his thoughts and observations on the Human Condition, Freedom, love, life and death, and everything in between, he creates works of Art in various media, including paintings, drawings, digital renderings using photographs and the multiple computer programs now available. Not one to limit himself or restrict his creativity to only one venue or resource, he works in whatever medium serves his Vision best. Oils, acrylics, pencil, and, of course, the pen. There is a metaphor in that for The Pen has now morphed into the keyboard of a computer. In today's world the mouse and the keystrokes of a keyboard make the metaphoric Pen even more powerful than ever before. In this age of computers and the internet his writings, both fiction and non-fiction, will see the light of day and be made available to the public through his websites and blogs, public forums, and social media sites. There will be more books to follow, and, no doubt, more Words In A Row.

www.ingramcontent.com/pod-product-compliance
Lightning Source LLC
Chambersburg PA
CBHW071807020426
42331CB00008B/2426